let's cook

chinese

Jenny
Stacey

p

Contents

Spring Rolls

This classic Chinese dish is very popular in the West .
Serve hot or chilled with a soy sauce or hoisin dip.

Serves 4

INGREDIENTS

175 g/6 oz cooked pork, chopped
75 g/2³⁄4 oz cooked chicken, chopped
1 tsp light soy sauce
1 tsp light brown sugar
1 tsp sesame oil
1 tsp vegetable oil
225 g/8 oz beansprouts

25 g/1 oz canned bamboo shoots,
   drained, rinsed and chopped
1 green (bell) pepper, seeded and chopped
2 spring onions (scallions), sliced
1 tsp cornflour (cornstarch)
2 tsp water
vegetable oil, for deep-frying

SKINS:
125 g/4¹⁄2 oz/1¹⁄8 cups plain (all-
   purpose) flour
5 tbsp cornflour (cornstarch)
450 ml/16 fl oz/2 cups water
3 tbsp vegetable oil

1 Mix the pork, chicken, soy sauce and sesame oil. Cover and marinate for 30 minutes.

2 Heat the oil in a preheated wok. Add the beansprouts, bamboo shoots, (bell) pepper and spring onions (scallions) and stir-fry for 2–3 minutes. Add the meat and the marinade to the wok and stir-fry for a further 2–3 minutes.

3 Blend the cornflour (cornstarch) with the water and stir the mixture into the wok. Set aside to cool completely.

4 To make the skins, mix the flour and cornflour (cornstarch) and gradually stir in the water, to make a smooth batter.

5 Heat a small, oiled frying pan (skillet). Swirl one-eighth of the batter over the base and cook for 2–3 minutes. Repeat with the remaining batter. Cover with a damp tea towel (dish cloth).

6 Spread out the skins and spoon one-eighth of the filling along the centre of each. Brush the edges with water and fold in the sides, then roll up.

7 Heat the oil for deep-frying in a wok to 180°C/350°F. Cook the spring rolls, in batches, for 2–3 minutes, or until golden and crisp. Remove from the oil with a slotted spoon and drain on absorbent kitchen paper (paper towels). Serve immediately.

Pork Dim Sum

*These small steamed parcels are traditionally served as an appetizer
and are very adaptable to your favourite fillings.*

Serves 4

INGREDIENTS

400 g/14 oz minced (ground) pork
2 spring onions (scallions), chopped
50 g/1³/4 oz canned bamboo shoots, drained, rinsed and chopped

1 tbsp light soy sauce
1 tbsp dry sherry
2 tsp sesame oil
2 tsp caster (superfine) sugar

1 egg white, lightly beaten
4¹/2 tsp cornflour (cornstarch)
24 wonton wrappers

1 Mix together the minced (ground) pork, spring onions (scallions), bamboo shoots, soy sauce, dry sherry, sesame oil, sugar and beaten egg white in a bowl until well combined.

2 Stir in the cornflour (cornstarch), mixing well.

3 Spread out the wonton wrappers on a work surface (counter). Place a spoonful of the pork and vegetable mixture in the centre of each wonton wrapper and lightly brush the edges of the wrappers with water.

4 Bring the sides of the wrappers together in the centre of the filling, pinching firmly together.

5 Line a steamer with a clean, damp tea towel (dish cloth) and arrange the wontons inside. Cover and steam for 5–7 minutes, until cooked through. Serve.

COOK'S TIP

Bamboo steamers are designed to rest on the sloping sides of a wok above the water. They are available in a range of sizes.

VARIATION

Use prawns (shrimp), minced (ground) chicken or crabmeat for the filling, with other vegetables, such as chopped carrot, and flavourings, such as chilli or ginger, if you prefer.

Szechuan White Fish

*Szechuan pepper is quite hot and should be used sparingly
to avoid making the dish unbearably spicy.*

Serves 4

INGREDIENTS

350 g/12 oz white fish fillets
1 small egg, beaten
3 tbsp plain (all-purpose) flour
4 tbsp dry white wine
3 tbsp light soy sauce
vegetable oil, for frying
1 garlic clove, cut into slivers

1-cm/^{1}/$_2$-inch piece fresh root
   ginger, finely chopped
1 onion, finely chopped
1 celery stick, chopped
1 fresh red chilli, chopped
3 spring onions (scallions), chopped
1 tsp rice wine vinegar

^{1}/$_2$ tsp ground Szechuan pepper
175 ml/6 fl oz/^{3}/$_4$ cup fish stock
1 tsp caster (superfine) sugar
1 tsp cornflour (cornstarch)
2 tsp water
chilli flowers and celery leaves,
   to garnish

1 Cut the fish into 4-cm/
1^1/$_2$-inch cubes.

2 In a mixing bowl, beat
together the egg, flour, wine
and 1 tablespoon of soy sauce to
make a batter.

3 Dip the cubes of fish into the
batter to coat well.

4 Heat the oil in a preheated
wok until it is almost
smoking. Reduce the heat slightly
and cook the fish, in batches, for
2–3 minutes, until golden brown.
Drain on kitchen paper (paper
towels), set aside and keep warm.

5 Pour all but 1 tablespoon of
oil from the wok and return
to the heat. Add the garlic, ginger,
onion, celery, chilli and spring
onions (scallions) and stir-fry for
1–2 minutes.

6 Stir in the remaining soy
sauce and the vinegar.

7 Add the Szechuan pepper, fish
stock and sugar to the wok.
Blend the cornflour (cornstarch)
with the water to form a smooth
paste and stir it into the stock.
Bring to the boil and cook,
stirring, for 1 minute, until the
sauce thickens and clears.

8 Return the fish to the wok
and cook for 1–2 minutes,
until hot. Transfer to a serving
dish, garnish with chilli flowers
and celery leaves and serve.

Lemon Chicken

This is on everyone's list of favourite Chinese dishes, and it is so simple to make. Fried chicken is cooked in a tangy lemon sauce in minutes and is great served with stir-fried vegetables.

Serves 4

INGREDIENTS

vegetable oil, for deep-frying
650 g/1¹/₂ lb skinless, boneless
   chicken, cut into strips
lemon slices and shredded spring
   onion (scallion), to garnish

SAUCE:
1 tbsp cornflour (cornstarch)
6 tbsp cold water
3 tbsp fresh lemon juice

2 tbsp sweet sherry
¹/₂ tsp caster (superfine) sugar

1 Heat the oil in a preheated wok until almost smoking. Reduce the heat and stir-fry the chicken strips for 3–4 minutes, until cooked through. Remove the chicken with a slotted spoon, set aside and keep warm. Drain the oil from the wok.

2 To make the sauce, mix the cornflour with 2 tablespoons of the water to form a paste.

3 Pour the lemon juice and remaining water into the mixture in the wok. Add the sherry and sugar and bring to the boil, stirring until the sugar has completely dissolved.

4 Stir in the cornflour mixture and return to the boil. Reduce the heat and simmer, stirring constantly, for 2-3 minutes, until the sauce is thickened and clear.

5 Transfer the chicken to a warm serving plate and pour the sauce over the top. Garnish with the lemon slices and shredded spring onion (scallion) and serve immediately.

COOK'S TIP

If you would prefer to use chicken portions rather than strips, cook them in the oil, covered, over a low heat for about 30 minutes, or until cooked through.

Chicken With Cashew Nuts & Vegetables

This is a popular dish in Chinese restaurants in the West,
although nothing beats making it yourself.

Serves 4

INGREDIENTS

300 g/10 1/2 oz boneless, skinless
    chicken breasts
1 tbsp cornflour (cornstarch)
1 tsp sesame oil
1 tbsp hoisin sauce
1 tsp light soy sauce
3 garlic cloves, crushed

2 tbsp vegetable oil
75 g/2 3/4 oz/3/4 cup unsalted
    cashew nuts
25 g/1 oz mangetout (snow peas)
1 celery stick, sliced
1 onion, cut into 8 pieces
60 g/2 oz beansprouts

1 red (bell) pepper, seeded and diced

SAUCE:
2 tsp cornflour (cornstarch)
2 tbsp hoisin sauce
200 ml/7 fl oz/7/8 cup chicken stock

1 Trim any fat from the chicken breasts and cut the meat into thin strips. Place the chicken in a large mixing bowl. Sprinkle with the cornflour (cornstarch) and toss to coat the chicken strips in it, shaking off any excess. Mix together the sesame oil, hoisin sauce, soy sauce and 1 garlic clove. Pour this mixture over the chicken, turning to coat thoroughly. Leave to marinate for 20 minutes.

2 Heat half of the vegetable oil in a preheated wok. Add the cashew nuts and stir-fry for 1 minute, until browned. Add the mangetout (snow peas), celery, the remaining garlic, the onion, beansprouts and red (bell) pepper and cook, stirring occasionally, for 2–3 minutes. Remove the vegetables from the wok with a slotted spoon, set aside and keep warm.

3 Heat the remaining oil in the wok. Remove the chicken from the marinade and stir-fry for 3–4 minutes. Return the vegetables to the wok.

4 To make the sauce, mix the cornflour (cornstarch), hoisin sauce and chicken stock together and pour into the wok. Bring to the boil, stirring until thickened and clear. Serve immediately.

Chicken Chop Suey

Both well known and popular, chop suey dishes are easy to make and delicious. They are based on beansprouts and soy sauce with a meat or vegetable flavouring.

Serves 4

INGREDIENTS

4 tbsp light soy sauce
2 tsp light brown sugar
500 g/1¼ lb skinless, boneless
   chicken breasts
3 tbsp vegetable oil

2 onions, quartered
2 garlic cloves, crushed
350 g/12 oz beansprouts
3 tsp sesame oil

1 tbsp cornflour (cornstarch)
3 tbsp water
425 ml/¾ pint/2 cups chicken stock
shredded leek, to garnish

1 Mix the soy sauce and sugar together, stirring until the sugar has dissolved.

2 Trim any fat from the chicken and cut the meat into thin strips. Place the chicken strips in a shallow glass dish and spoon the soy mixture over them, turning to coat. Leave to marinate in the refrigerator for 20 minutes.

3 Heat the oil in a preheated wok. Add the chicken and stir-fry for 2–3 minutes, until golden brown.

4 Add the onions and garlic and cook for a further 2 minutes. Add the beansprouts, cook for a further 4–5 minutes, then add the sesame oil.

5 Blend the cornflour (cornstarch) with the water to form a smooth paste. Pour the stock into the wok, together with the cornflour (cornstarch) paste and bring to the boil, stirring constantly until the sauce is thickened and clear. Transfer to a warm serving dish, garnish with shredded leek and serve immediately.

VARIATION

This recipe may be made with strips of lean steak, pork or with mixed vegetables. Change the type of stock accordingly.

Peking Duck

No Chinese cookery book would be complete without this famous recipe. Crispy skinned duck is served with pancakes and a tangy sauce for a really special meal.

Serves 4

INGREDIENTS

1.8 kg/4 lb duck
1.75 litres/3 pints/7^1/$_2$ cups boiling water
4 tbsp clear honey
2 tsp dark soy sauce

2 tbsp sesame oil
125 ml/4 fl oz/^{1}/$_2$ cup hoisin sauce
125 g/4^1/$_2$ oz/^{2}/$_3$ cup caster (superfine) sugar
125 ml/4 fl oz/^{1}/$_2$ cup water

carrot strips, to garnish
Chinese pancakes, cucumber matchsticks and spring onions (scallions), to serve

1 Place the duck on a rack set over a roasting tin (pan) and pour 1.2 litres/2 pints/5 cups of the boiling water over it. Remove the duck and rack and discard the water. Pat dry with paper towels, replace the duck and the rack and set aside for several hours.

2 Mix together the honey, remaining boiling water and soy sauce. Brush the mixture over the skin and inside the duck. Reserve the remaining glaze. Set the duck aside for 1 hour, until the glaze has dried.

3 Coat the duck with another layer of glaze. Let dry and repeat until all of the glaze is used.

4 Heat the oil and add the hoisin sauce, sugar and water. Simmer for 2–3 minutes, until thickened. Cool and refrigerate.

5 Cook the duck in a preheated oven, at 190°C/375°F/Gas Mark 5, for 30 minutes. Turn the duck over and cook for 20 minutes. Turn the duck again and cook for 20–30 minutes, or until cooked through and the skin is crisp.

6 Remove the duck from the oven and set aside for 10 minutes. Meanwhile, heat the pancakes in a steamer for 5–7 minutes. Cut the skin and duck meat into strips, garnish with the carrot strips and serve with the pancakes, sauce, cucumber and spring onions (scallions).

COOK'S TIP

Keep the pancakes covered while working to prevent them from drying out.

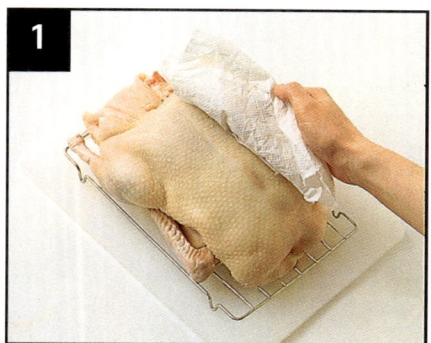

Pork Fry with Vegetables

This is a very simple dish which lends itself to almost any combination of vegetables that you have to hand.

Serves 4

INGREDIENTS

350 g/12 oz lean pork
   fillet (tenderloin)
2 tbsp vegetable oil
2 garlic cloves, crushed
1-cm/^{1}/$_2$-inch piece fresh root
   ginger, cut into slivers

1 carrot, cut into thin strips
1 red (bell) pepper, seeded and diced
1 fennel bulb, sliced
25 g/1 oz water chestnuts, halved
75 g/2 ^{3}/$_4$ oz beansprouts
2 tbsp Chinese rice wine

300 ml/^{1}/$_2$ pint/1^1/$_4$ cups pork or
   chicken stock
pinch of dark brown sugar
1 tsp cornflour (cornstarch)
2 tsp water

1 Cut the pork into thin slices. Heat the oil in a preheated wok. Add the garlic, ginger and pork and stir-fry for 1–2 minutes, until the meat is sealed.

2 Add the carrot, (bell) pepper, fennel and water chestnuts to the wok and stir-fry for about 2-3 minutes.

3 Add the beansprouts and stir-fry for 1 minute. Remove the pork and vegetables from the wok and keep warm.

4 Add the Chinese rice wine, pork or chicken stock and sugar to the wok. Blend the cornflour (cornstarch) to a smooth paste with the water and stir it into the sauce. Bring to the boil, stirring constantly until thickened and clear.

5 Return the meat and vegetables to the wok and cook for 1–2 minutes, until heated through and coated with the sauce. Transfer to a warm serving dish and serve immediately.

COOK'S TIP

Use dry sherry instead of the Chinese rice wine if you have difficulty obtaining it.

Sweet & Sour Pork

*This dish is a popular choice in Western diets, and must be one
of the best known of Chinese recipes.*

Serves 4

INGREDIENTS

150 ml/^{1}/4 pint/^{2}/3 cup vegetable oil,
 for deep-frying
225 g/8 oz pork fillet (tenderloin), cut
 into 1-cm/^{1}/2-inch cubes
1 onion, sliced
1 green (bell) pepper, seeded
 and sliced
225 g/8 oz pineapple pieces
1 small carrot, cut into thin strips

25 g/1 oz canned bamboo shoots,
 drained, rinsed and halved
rice or noodles, to serve

BATTER:
125 g/4^1/2 oz/1 cup plain (all-
 purpose) flour
1 tbsp cornflour (cornstarch)
1^1/2 tsp baking powder
1 tbsp vegetable oil

SAUCE:
125 g/4^1/2 oz/^{2}/3 cup light brown
 sugar
2 tbsp cornflour (cornstarch)
125 ml/4 fl oz/^{1}/2 cup white
 wine vinegar
2 garlic cloves, crushed
4 tbsp tomato purée (paste)
6 tbsp pineapple juice

1 To make the batter, sift the flour into a mixing bowl, together with the cornflour (cornstarch) and baking powder. Add the oil and stir in enough water to make a thick, smooth batter (about 175 ml/6 fl oz/ ^{3}/4 cup).

2 Pour the vegetable oil into a wok and heat until almost smoking. Dip the cubes of pork into the batter, and cook in the hot oil, in batches, until the pork is cooked through. Remove the pork from the wok with a slotted spoon, set aside and keep warm.

3 Drain all but 1 tablespoon of oil from the wok and return it to the heat. Add the onion, (bell) pepper, pineapple pieces, carrot and bamboo shoots and stir-fry for 1–2 minutes. Remove from the wok with a slotted spoon and set aside.

4 Mix all of the sauce ingredients together and pour into the wok. Bring to the boil, stirring until thickened and clear. Cook for 1 minute, then return the pork and vegetables to the wok. Cook for a further 1–2 minutes, then transfer to a serving plate and serve with rice or noodles.

Beef & Broccoli Stir-fry

*This is a great combination of ingredients in terms of colour and flavour,
and it is so simple and quick to prepare.*

Serves 4

INGREDIENTS

225 g/8 oz lean steak, trimmed
2 garlic cloves, crushed
dash of chilli oil
1-cm/^{1}/$_2$-inch piece fresh root
  ginger, grated

^{1}/$_2$ tsp Chinese five spice powder
2 tbsp dark soy sauce
2 tbsp vegetable oil
150 g/5 oz broccoli florets
1 tbsp light soy sauce

150 ml/^{1}/$_4$ pint/^{2}/$_3$ cup beef stock
2 tsp cornflour (cornstarch)
4 tsp water
carrot strips, to garnish

1 Cut the steak into thin strips and place in a shallow glass dish. Mix together the garlic, chilli oil, grated ginger, Chinese five spice powder and soy sauce in a small bowl and pour over the beef, tossing to coat the strips evenly. Leave to marinate in the refrigerator.

2 Heat 1 tablespoon of the vegetable oil in a preheated wok. Add the broccoli and stir-fry over a medium heat for 4–5 minutes. Remove from the wok with a slotted spoon and set aside.

3 Heat the remaining oil in the wok. Add the steak together with the marinade, and stir-fry for 2-3 minutes, until the steak is browned and sealed.

4 Return the broccoli to the wok and stir in the soy sauce and stock.

5 Blend the cornflour (cornstarch) with the water to form a smooth paste and stir it into the wok. Bring to the boil, stirring, until thickened and clear. Cook for 1 minute.

6 Transfer the beef and broccoli stir-fry to a warm serving dish, arrange the carrot strips in a lattice on top and serve immediately.

COOK'S TIP

Leave the steak to marinate for several hours for a fuller flavour. Cover and leave to marinate in the refrigerator if preparing in advance.

Spicy Beef

In this recipe beef is marinated in a five-spice and chilli marinade for a spicy flavour.

Serves 4

INGREDIENTS

225 g/8 oz fillet steak
2 garlic cloves, crushed
1 tsp powdered star anise
1 tbsp dark soy sauce
spring onion (scallion) tassels, to
  garnish

SAUCE:
2 tbsp vegetable oil
1 bunch spring onions (scallions),
  halved lengthways
1 tbsp dark soy sauce

1 tbsp dry sherry
$^1/_4$ tsp chilli sauce
150 ml/$^1/_4$ pint/$^2/_3$ cup water
2 tsp cornflour (cornstarch)
4 tsp water

1 Cut the steak into thin strips and place in a shallow dish.

2 Mix together the garlic, star anise and dark soy sauce in a bowl and pour over the steak strips, turning them to coat thoroughly. Cover and leave to marinate in the refrigerator for at least 1 hour.

3 Heat the oil in a preheated wok. Reduce the heat, add the halved spring onions (scallions) and stir-fry for 1-2 minutes. Remove from the wok with a slotted spoon and set aside.

4 Add the beef to the wok, together with the marinade, and stir-fry for 3–4 minutes. Return the halved spring onions (scallions) to the wok and add the soy sauce, sherry, chilli sauce and two thirds of the water.

5 Blend the cornflour (cornstarch) with the remaining water and stir into the wok. Bring to the boil, stirring until the sauce thickens and clears.

6 Transfer to a warm serving dish, garnish with spring onion (scallion) tassels and serve immediately.

COOK'S TIP

Omit the chilli sauce for a milder dish.

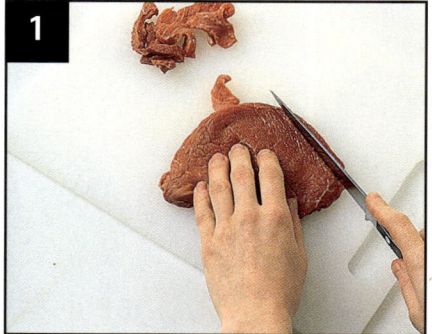

Lamb with Mushroom Sauce

*Use a lean cut of lamb, such as fillet, for this recipe
for both flavour and tenderness.*

Serves 4

INGREDIENTS

350 g/12 oz lean boneless lamb, such
  as fillet or loin
2 tbsp vegetable oil
3 garlic cloves, crushed
1 leek, sliced
1 tsp cornflour (cornstarch)

4 tbsp light soy sauce
3 tbsp Chinese rice wine or
  dry sherry
3 tbsp water
$^1/_2$ tsp chilli sauce
175 g/6 oz large mushrooms, sliced

$^1/_2$ tsp sesame oil
fresh red chillies, to garnish

---

1 Using a sharp knife, cut the lamb into thin strips.

2 Heat the oil in a preheated wok. Add the lamb strips, garlic and leek and stir-fry for about 2-3 minutes.

3 Mix together the cornflour (cornstarch), soy sauce, Chinese rice wine or dry sherry, water and chilli sauce in a bowl and set aside.

4 Add the mushrooms to the wok and stir-fry for 1 minute.

5 Stir in the sauce and cook for 2–3 minutes, or until the lamb is cooked through and tender. Sprinkle the sesame oil over the top and transfer to a warm serving dish. Garnish with red chillies and serve immediately.

COOK'S TIP

Use rehydrated dried Chinese mushrooms obtainable from specialist shops or Chinese supermarkets for a really authentic flavour.

VARIATION

The lamb can be replaced with lean steak or pork fillet (tenderloin) in this classic recipe from Beijing. You could also use 2–3 spring onions (scallions), 1 shallot or 1 small onion instead of the leek, if you prefer.

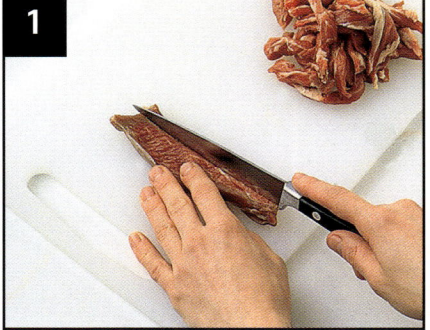

Sesame Lamb Stir-Fry

This is a very simple, but delicious dish, in which lean pieces of lamb are cooked in sugar and soy sauce and sprinkled with sesame seeds, then served on a bed of leeks and carrot.

Serves 4

INGREDIENTS

450 g/1 lb boneless lean lamb
2 tbsp peanut oil
2 leeks, sliced
1 carrot, cut into matchsticks

2 garlic cloves, crushed
3 fl oz/85 ml/$\frac{1}{3}$ cup lamb or
  vegetable stock
2 tsp light brown sugar

1 tbsp dark soy sauce
4$\frac{1}{2}$ tsp sesame seeds

1   Cut the lamb into thin strips. Heat the peanut oil in a preheated wok. Add the lamb and stir-fry for 2–3 minutes. Remove the lamb from the wok with a slotted spoon and set aside.

2   Add the leek, carrot and garlic to the wok and stir-fry in the remaining oil for 1–2 minutes. Remove from the wok with a slotted spoon and set aside. Drain any remaining oil from the wok.

3   Place the lamb or vegetable stock, sugar and soy sauce in the wok and add the lamb. Cook, stirring constantly to coat the lamb, for 2–3 minutes. Sprinkle the sesame seeds over the top, turning the lamb to coat.

4   Spoon the leek mixture on to a warm serving dish and top with the lamb. Serve immediately.

VARIATION

This recipe would be equally delicious made with strips of skinless chicken or turkey breast or with prawns (shrimp). The cooking times remain the same.

COOK'S TIP

Be careful not to burn the sugar in the wok when heating and coating the meat, otherwise the flavour of the dish will be spoiled.

Marinated Beansprouts & Vegetables

This dish is served cold as a salad or appetizer and is very easy to make. It is a form of cold chop suey.

Serves 4

INGREDIENTS

450 g/1 lb beansprouts
2 fresh red chillies, seeded and finely
   chopped
1 red (bell) pepper, seeded and
   thinly sliced

1 green (bell) pepper, seeded and
   thinly sliced
60 g/2 oz water chestnuts, quartered
1 celery stick, sliced
3 tbsp rice wine vinegar

2 tbsp light soy sauce
2 tbsp chopped chives
1 garlic clove, crushed
pinch of Chinese curry powder

1 Place the beansprouts, chilli, (bell) peppers, water chestnuts and celery in a large bowl and mix well.

2 Mix together the rice wine vinegar, soy sauce, chives, garlic and Chinese curry powder in a bowl and pour over the prepared vegetables. Toss to mix thoroughly.

3 Cover the salad and leave to chill for at least 3 hours. Drain the vegetables thoroughly, transfer to a serving dish and serve.

COOK'S TIP

There are hundreds of varieties of chillies and it is not always possible to tell how hot they are going to be. As a general rule, dark green chillies are hotter than light green and red chillies. Thin, pointed chillies are usually hotter than fatter, blunter chillies. However, there are always exceptions and even chillies from the same plant can vary considerably in their degree of spiciness. The heat of chillies is measured in Scoville units.

COOK'S TIP

This dish is delicious with Chinese roasted meats or served with the marinade and noodles.

Green Stir-fry

*The basis of this recipe is pak choi, sometimes known as bok choy or Chinese greens.
If unavailable, use Swiss chard or Savoy cabbage instead.*

Serves 4

INGREDIENTS

2 tbsp peanut oil
2 garlic cloves, crushed
$^{1}/_{2}$ tsp ground star anise
1 tsp salt

350 g/12 oz pak choi, shredded
225 g/8 oz baby spinach
25 g/1 oz mangetout (snow peas)
1 celery stick, sliced

1 green (bell) pepper, seeded
  and sliced
50 ml/2 fl oz/$^{1}/_{4}$ cup vegetable stock
1 tsp sesame oil

---

1 Heat the peanut oil in a preheated wok.

2 Add the crushed garlic to the wok and stir-fry for about 30 seconds. Stir in the star anise, salt, pak choi, spinach, mangetout (snow peas), celery and green (bell) pepper and stir-fry for 3–4 minutes.

3 Add the stock, cover and cook for 3–4 minutes.

4 Remove the lid from the wok and stir in the sesame oil. Mix thoroughly.

5 Transfer the stir-fry to a warm serving dish and serve.

COOK'S TIP

Star anise is an important ingredient in Chinese cuisine. The attractive star-shaped pods are often used whole to add a decorative garnish to dishes. The flavour is similar to liquorice, but with spicy undertones and is quite strong. Together with cassia, cloves, fennel seeds and Szechuan pepper, dried star anise is used to make Chinese five spice powder.

COOK'S TIP

Serve this dish as part of a vegetarian meal or alternatively, with roast meats.

Vegetable Chop Suey

Make sure that the vegetables are all cut into pieces of a similar size in this recipe, so that they cook within the same amount of time.

Serves 4

INGREDIENTS

1 yellow (bell) pepper, seeded
1 red (bell) pepper, seeded
1 carrot
1 courgette (zucchini)
1 fennel bulb
1 onion

60 g/2 oz mangetout (snow peas)
2 tbsp peanut oil
3 garlic cloves, crushed
1 tsp grated fresh root ginger
125 g/4^1/2 oz beansprouts
2 tsp light brown sugar

2 tbsp light soy sauce
125 ml/4 fl oz/^{1}/2 cup vegetable
 stock

1 Cut the (bell) peppers, carrot, courgette (zucchini) and fennel into thin slices. Cut the onion into quarters and then cut each quarter in half. Slice the mangetout (snow peas) diagonally to create the maximum surface area.

2 Heat the oil in a preheated wok until it is almost smoking. Add the garlic and ginger and stir-fry for 30 seconds. Add the onion and stir-fry for a further 30 seconds.

3 Add the (bell) peppers, carrot, courgette (zucchini), fennel and mangetout (snow peas) to the wok and stir-fry for 2 minutes.

4 Add the beansprouts to the wok and stir in the sugar, soy sauce and stock. Reduce the heat to low and simmer for 1–2 minutes, until the vegetables are tender and coated in the sauce.

5 Transfer the vegetables and sauce to a serving dish and serve immediately.

COOK'S TIP

Use any combination of colourful vegetables that you have to hand to make this versatile dish.

Chinese Vegetable Casserole

This mixed vegetable casserole is very versatile and is delicious with any combination of vegetables of your choice.

Serves 4

INGREDIENTS

4 tbsp vegetable oil
2 medium carrots, sliced
1 courgette (zucchini), sliced
4 baby corn cobs, halved lengthways
125 g/4^1/$_2$ oz cauliflower florets
1 leek, sliced

125 g/4^1/$_2$ oz water chestnuts, halved
225 g/8 oz tofu (bean curd), diced
300 ml/^{1}/$_2$ pint/1^1/$_4$ cups vegetable stock
1 tsp salt
2 tsp dark brown sugar

2 tsp dark soy sauce
2 tbsp dry sherry
1 tbsp cornflour (cornstarch)
2 tbsp water
1 tbsp chopped coriander (cilantro), to garnish

1 Heat the vegetable oil in a preheated wok until it is almost smoking.

2 Lower the heat slightly, add the carrots, courgette (zucchini), corn cobs, cauliflower florets and leek to the wok and stir-fry for 2–3 minutes.

3 Stir in the water chestnuts, tofu (bean curd), stock, salt, sugar, soy sauce and sherry and bring to the boil. Reduce the heat, cover and simmer for 20 minutes.

4 Blend the cornflour (cornstarch) with the water to form a smooth paste.

5 Remove the lid from the wok and stir in the cornflour (cornstarch) mixture. Bring the sauce to the boil and cook, stirring constantly until it thickens and clears.

6 Transfer the casserole to a warm serving dish, sprinkle with chopped coriander (cilantro) and serve immediately.

COOK'S TIP

If there is too much liquid remaining, boil vigorously for 1 minute before adding the cornflour (cornstarch) to reduce it slightly.

Bamboo Shoots, Ginger & (Bell) Peppers

This dish has a wonderfully strong ginger flavour which is integral to Chinese cooking. The mixed (bell) peppers give the otherwise insipid bamboo shoots a burst of colour.

Serves 4

INGREDIENTS

2 tbsp peanut oil
225 g/8 oz canned bamboo shoots, drained and rinsed
2.5-cm/1-inch piece fresh root ginger, finely chopped
1 small red (bell) pepper, seeded and thinly sliced

1 small green (bell) pepper, seeded and thinly sliced
1 small yellow (bell) pepper, seeded and thinly sliced
1 leek, sliced
125 ml/4 fl oz/$^{1}/_{2}$ cup vegetable stock

1 tbsp light soy sauce
2 tsp light brown sugar
2 tsp Chinese rice wine or dry sherry
1 tsp cornflour (cornstarch)
2 tsp water
1 tsp sesame oil

1 Heat the peanut oil in a preheated wok.

2 Add the bamboo shoots, ginger, (bell) peppers and leek to the wok and stir-fry for 2–3 minutes.

3 Stir in the stock, soy sauce, sugar and Chinese rice wine or sherry and bring to the boil, stirring. Reduce the heat and simmer for 4–5 minutes, or until the vegetables begin to soften.

4 Blend the cornflour (cornstarch) with the water to form a smooth paste.

5 Stir the cornflour (cornstarch) paste into the wok. Bring to the boil and cook, stirring constantly, until the sauce thickens and clears.

6 Sprinkle the sesame oil over the vegetables and cook for 1 minute. Transfer to a warm serving dish and serve immediately.

COOK'S TIP

Add a chopped fresh red chilli or a few drops of chilli sauce for a spicier dish.

Special Fried Rice

This dish is a popular choice in Chinese restaurants. Ham and prawns (shrimp)
are mixed with vegetables in a soy-flavoured rice.

Serves 4

INGREDIENTS

150 g/5¹/₂ oz/²/₃ cup long-grain rice
2 tbsp vegetable oil
2 eggs, beaten
2 garlic cloves, crushed

1 tsp grated fresh root ginger
3 spring onions (scallions), sliced
75 g/3 oz/³/₄ cup cooked peas
150 g/5¹/₂ oz/²/₃ cup beansprouts

225 g/8 oz/1¹/₃ cups shredded ham
150 g/5¹/₂ oz peeled, cooked prawns
  (shrimp)
2 tbsp light soy sauce

1 Cook the rice in a saucepan of boiling water for about 15 minutes. Drain well, rinse under cold water and drain thoroughly again.

2 Heat 1 tablespoon of the oil in a preheated wok and add the beaten eggs and a further 1 teaspoon of oil. Tilt the wok so that the egg covers the base to make a thin pancake. Cook until lightly browned on the underside, then flip the pancake over and cook on the other side for 1 minute. Remove from the wok and leave to cool.

3 Heat the remaining oil in the wok. Add the garlic and ginger and stir-fry for 30 seconds.

4 Add the spring onions (scallions), peas, beansprouts, ham and prawns (shrimp) to the wok and stir-fry for 2 minutes.

5 Stir in the soy sauce and rice and cook for a further 2 minutes. Transfer the rice to serving dishes.

6 Roll up the pancake, slice it very thinly and use to garnish the rice. Serve immediately.

COOK'S TIP

As this recipe contains meat and fish, it is ideal served with simpler vegetable dishes.

Noodles with Prawns (Shrimp)

This is a simple dish using egg noodles and large prawns (shrimp), which give the dish a wonderful flavour, texture and colour.

Serves 4

INGREDIENTS

225 g/8 oz thin egg noodles
2 tbsp peanut oil
1 garlic clove, crushed
1/2 tsp ground star anise

1 bunch spring onions (scallions), cut into 5-cm/2-inch pieces
24 raw tiger prawns (jumbo shrimp), peeled with tails intact

2 tbsp light soy sauce
2 tsp lime juice
lime wedges, to garnish

1 Blanch the noodles in a saucepan of boiling water for about 2 minutes. Drain well, rinse under cold water and drain thoroughly again.

2 Heat the oil in a preheated wok until almost smoking.

3 Add the garlic and star anise to the wok and stir-fry for 30 seconds.

4 Add the spring onions (scallions) and prawns (shrimp) to the wok and stir-fry for 2-3 minutes.

5 Stir in the soy sauce, lime juice and noodles and mix well. Cook for 1 minute, then spoon into a warm serving dish. Transfer to serving bowls, garnish with lime wedges and serve immediately.

COOK'S TIP

Chinese egg noodles are made from wheat or rice flour, water and egg. Noodles are a symbol of longevity, and so are always served at birthday celebrations – it is regarded as bad luck to cut them.

VARIATION

This dish is just as tasty with smaller cooked prawns (shrimp), but it is not quite so visually appealing.

Beef Chow Mein

Chow Mein must be the best-known and most popular noodle dish on any Chinese menu. Beef is used in this recipe, but you could use chicken, pork or vegetables instead.

Serves 4

INGREDIENTS

450 g/1 lb egg noodles
4 tbsp peanut oil
450 g/1 lb lean beef steak, cut into thin strips
2 garlic cloves, crushed

1 tsp grated fresh root ginger
1 green (bell) pepper, thinly sliced
1 carrot, thinly sliced
2 celery sticks, sliced
8 spring onions (scallions)

1 tsp dark brown sugar
1 tbsp dry sherry
2 tbsp dark soy sauce
few drops of chilli sauce

1 Cook the noodles in a saucepan of boiling salted water for 4-5 minutes. Drain well, rinse under cold running water and drain thoroughly again.

2 Toss the noodles in 1 tablespoon of the oil.

3 Heat the remaining oil in a preheated wok. Add the beef and stir-fry for 3-4 minutes, stirring constantly.

4 Add the garlic and ginger and stir-fry for 30 seconds.

5 Add the (bell) pepper, carrot, celery and spring onions (scallions) and stir-fry for about 2 minutes.

6 Add the sugar, sherry, soy sauce and chilli sauce and cook, stirring, for 1 minute.

7 Stir in the noodles, mixing well, and cook until completely warmed through.

8 Transfer the noodles to warm serving bowls and serve immediately.

VARIATION

A variety of different vegetables may be used in this recipe for colour and flavour – try broccoli, red (bell) peppers, green beans or baby sweetcorn cobs.

Egg Fried Rice

This is a classic Chinese rice dish which has become very popular in the Western diet. Boiled rice is fried with peas, spring onions (scallions) and egg and flavoured with soy sauce.

Serves 4

INGREDIENTS

150 g/5^1/$_2$ oz/^{2}/$_3$ cup long-grain rice
3 eggs, beaten
2 tbsp vegetable oil
2 garlic cloves, crushed

4 spring onions (scallions), chopped
125 g/4^1/$_2$ oz/1 cup cooked peas
1 tbsp light soy sauce

pinch of salt
shredded spring onion (scallion), to
   garnish

1 Cook the rice in a saucepan of boiling water for 10-12 minutes, until almost cooked, but not soft. Drain well, rinse under cold water and drain thoroughly again.

2 Place the beaten eggs in a saucepan and cook over a gentle heat, stirring until softly scrambled.

3 Heat the oil in a preheated wok. Add the garlic, spring onions (scallions) and peas and sauté, stirring occasionally, for 1-2 minutes.

4 Stir the rice into the mixture in the pan, mixing to combine.

5 Add the eggs, soy sauce and salt to the wok and stir to mix the egg in thoroughly.

6 Transfer to serving dishes and serve garnished with the shredded spring onion (scallion).

VARIATION

You may choose to add prawns (shrimp), ham or chicken in step 3, if you wish.

COOK'S TIP

The rice is rinsed under cold water to wash out the starch and prevent it from sticking together.

This is a Parragon Publishing Book
First published in 2003

Parragon Publishing
Queen Street House
4 Queen Street, Bath, BA1 1HE, UK

Copyright © Parragon 2003

All recipes and photography compiled from material
created by 'Haldane Mason', and 'The Foundry'.

Cover design by Shelley Doyle.

ISBN: 1-40540-841-3

Printed in China

NOTE

Cup measurements in this book are for American cups. This book uses
imperial and metric measurements. Follow the same units of measurement
throughout; do not mix imperial and metric. All spoon measurements are
level; teaspoons are assumed to be 5 ml and tablespoons are assumed to be
15 ml. Unless otherwise stated, milk is assumed to be whole milk, eggs
and individual vegetables such as potatoes are medium, and pepper is
freshly ground black pepper.

The times given for each recipe are an approximate guide only because
the preparation times may differ according to the techniques used by
different people and the cooking times may vary as a result of the
type of oven used.

Recipes using raw or very lightly cooked eggs should be avoided by
infants, the elderly, pregnant women, convalescents and anyone
suffering from an illness.